Living Rooms

Living Rooms

Coleen Cahill

HEARST BOOKS

A Division of Sterling Publishing Co., Inc.

New York

A Primrose Production
Designed by Niloo Tehranchi

The Library of Congress has catalogued the hardcover edition as follows:
Cahill, Coleen.
   Country living : living rooms / by Coleen Cahill.
        p. cm. -- (Easy transformations)
   ISBN 1-58816-287-7
   1. Living rooms. 2. Interior decoration. I. Title. II. Series.
   NK2117.L5C34 2003
   747.7'5--dc21
2003005422

10 9 8 7 6 5 4 3 2 1

First Paperback Edition 2005
Published by Hearst Books
A Division of Sterling Publishing Co., Inc.
387 Park Avenue South, New York, NY 10016

www.countryliving.com

For information about custom editions, special sales, premium and corporate purchases, please contact Sterling Special Sales Department at 800-805-5489 or specialsales@sterlingpub.com.

Distributed in Canada by Sterling Publishing
c/o Canadian Manda Group, 165 Dufferin Street
Toronto, Ontario, Canada M6K 3H6

Distributed in Australia by Capricorn Link (Australia) Pty. Ltd.
P.O. Box 704, Windsor, NSW 2756 Australia

Manufactured in China

ISBN 1-58816-503-5

Contents

Foreword

"What makes it country?" is a question I'm frequently asked. For me, the true appeal of country style is that it has no distinct definition. It is a relaxed, comfortable decorating style that is adaptable for any type of home, regardless of its age or location. It is a look that mixes old and new in creative, and sometimes, surprising ways. And it demands personalization—something that makes it truly distinctive for each and every homeowner.

In this book, we examine the popularity of today's country style in one of the most important rooms of the house—the living room. Over the years we have seen the living room evolve from a somewhat formal space reserved for special occasions and entertaining to a "Great Room" brimming with a full range of family activities. Nowhere has the challenge of good design been more apparent, or the comfort of country style more appropriate.

In the pages that follow you will see how others have interpreted the country look in their homes and how easily you can too. See how color can transform any room—even if the color you choose is white. Find simple ways to add pattern and texture with vintage quilts, woolen throws and decorative pillows you can make. Learn how furniture arrangement can actually enhance the function of a room—defining areas within an open floor plan or making a small space appear larger.

Since country style is all about mixing old and new, don't overlook inventive uses for old objects, like baskets for practical storage solutions, old benches as side or coffee tables, and vintage store signs and game boards as wall art. If you are saddled with a mismatched chair and sofa, slipcovers can provide a quick and stylish solution. Don't overlook elegant accents either—a crystal chandelier or period style chaise can make quite a statement in a country space. And, if you are a collector (and who among us isn't), there are great examples for storing, displaying and living with the things you love.

With home entertainment a necessary requirement in today's family room, see how adaptable country style is for storing and concealing TVs, DVDs, and home theater components. There are stylish options to suit your specific needs, from built-in cabinets to retrofitted flea market finds to newly manufactured, country-style entertainment cabinets.

Whether you are looking for a quick and easy way to freshen your existing living room or considering a complete makeover, this book will provide plenty of inspiration and advice to help you realize your dreams. "What makes it country?" When all is said and done—you do!

NANCY SORIANO
Editor-in-Chief
Country Living Magazine

ABOVE: When the seasons change, it's a perfect time to think about refreshing your living room. This already sunny space is lightened by a pale green color on the walls that creates a sense of calm. Introducing new color into a space is one of the simplest ways to transform the mood of any room.

Introduction

The architectural style or exterior of a home is often a clear marker of when the house was built or the time period that it has been designed to recapture. In a far less public way, the interiors of homes have also evolved to reflect changing times. Recently, the living room in particular has undergone a redefinition.

Often in today's homes, some form of "great room"—which combines kitchen, dining and living areas into one space—has replaced the traditional living and/or family room. Openess is one of the most desirable aspects of a great room, which also allows the whole family to enjoy the same space while performing different activities. Kids can focus on projects or homework at the kitchen table, while parents relax in the living area. When you entertain in a great room, you can put the finishing touches on dinner while still conversing with guests.

In older homes, you'll frequently still find a formal living room and a less formal family room or den. Many homes—both old and new—rely on a single room as the living space for the entire family. In these cases, the challenge is creating a room or rooms that can accommodate all the things your family does, and evolve as your family's needs change. Of course, sometimes you're ready for a change in style even if your needs haven't changed.

Easy Transformations: *Living Rooms* offers ideas and solutions to the challenges of making your living area work for your life and your entire family. The examples you will find in the following pages are all real rooms that live up to the demands of today's lifestyles. Each of them also expresses the country aesthetic in a highly individual way. Let these images and ideas inspire you to create the living space that suits you and your family. Use the practical tips to achieve your transformation—whether minor or major—and enjoy the results!

RIGHT: Lose your inhibitions when looking to make a dramatic personal statement in your living room. Mix furnishings from different periods for a completely original take on country. This room combines antique chairs with leopard fabric, a dripping chandelier, and a truly unique table base for an eclectic look.

Country Comfort

Today's lifestyles demand that living rooms offer both comfort and good looks. Among country style's great charms is its ability to accommodate family and friends comfortably, yet without sacrificing style. The key here is to choose the right seating pieces. Overstuffed chairs and deep-cushioned sofas are featured in a wide variety of styles, and in fabrics that are durable enough to stand up to everyday use. Slipcovers let you change the look of your sofa or chairs seasonally or from day into evening. When you want to raise the comfort quotient of your living room right away, think pillows—and lots of them!

RIGHT: Color and pattern combined are a country staple; in this cheerful living room stylish comfort is the number one priority. The sofa features four different fabrics: a quilted neutral for the back and sides of the sofa, stripes for the bottom cushion, a rich hue for the back bolster, and an elegant print for the throw pillow. The stripes are reprised nearby on a pair of upholstered chairs, and a generous ottoman is upholstered to match the bolster and cushioned for extra comfort.

A TEXTURED CARPET DRAWS ALL THE ELEMENTS TOGETHER, AND SOFTENS THE HARDWOOD FLOORS.

DRAPES ADD WARMTH TO THE ROOM—LITERALLY.
LINED WITH THE SAME QUILTED FABRIC AS THE
SOFA, THEY PROTECT AGAINST DRAFTS AS WELL
AS WARM UP THE ROOM VISUALLY.

ABOVE: Don't be afraid to mix and match fabrics on one piece. Then pick up those fabrics in other places throughout the room—each fabric should appear at least twice. Don't worry about exact matches; the toile curtains and pillow work because they are within the same family.

A B O V E : A Victorian wool quilt—a Fans variation—
hangs above the sofa, adding coziness and a folksy
feel to this space. The neatly tailored sofa is
enhanced by a collection of pillows in antique florals
that can accommodate different stages of relaxation.

NEEDLEPOINT PILLOWS ADD COLOR AND
TEXTURE TO THE SOFA; AS HANDWORKED
ART, THEY ALSO RELATE TO THE QUILT.

ABOVE: Layers of wool offer both comfort and warmth, especially during the winter months. As the cold weather approaches, transform your sofa into a welcoming refuge with wool throws and pillows that are soft and inviting. Drape a nearby table with a wintry throw to complete the look. Accessories offer simple and quick ways to transition a room from one season to the next.

RIGHT: Country style takes its cues from nature. Natural hues, varied textures, and subtle plaids in a fall palette combine for a stylish effect.

Make a Quick Change

Decorate with vintage china plates. Why not dust off your grandmother's china and select a few special pieces than can be displayed in your living room? Either hang them on the wall using wire plate hangers (which are widely available) or present them in plate stands on the mantel. Don't worry about pieces matching exactly—mix and match patterns, colors, and sizes for an eclectic effect.

LEFT: Fabric used on the fireplace surround adds another layer of interest while echoing the subtle textures and hues throughout the room.

ABOVE: Comfortable furniture arranged around the focal points of this room—the hearth and round coffee table—contribute to the relaxed elegance. The sofa and armchairs were given new life after being restuffed and reupholstered in muslin and natural linen. The leather bench is a flea market find fitted with a tufted cushion covered in soft chenille—matching bolsters on either end add even more comfort.

Make a Pillow

Basic throw pillows vary in size from 16 inches to 24 inches square. These instructions are for the smaller size; adjust all measurements to reflect the desired size of your pillow.

1. Using tailor's chalk, outline a square on the fabric, allowing an extra $1/2$-inch on all sides. If your pillow is 18 inches square, mark the fabric to create an 18 $1/2$" by 18 $1/2$" square. Cut the fabric along the chalked line.

2. Pin the two right sides of the fabric together with at least $1/2$" seam allowance. Pin three sides only.

3. Machine-sew the three sides together, then trim seams and clip corners.

4. Turn the pillow right side out. Press.

5. Insert pillow, and hand stitch the opening or insert a zipper or button closure.

Try using two different fabrics for front and back. Or make a color-block pillow that features two different colors on one side or both sides of the pillow. For more embellishment, add trim or tufting to your pillow. You can also explore different closures such as ribbons, buttons, and even Velcro!

R I G H T : An assortment of brightly hued pillows adds color to this neutral sofa and raises the comfort quotient at the same time. Pillows are a simple way to add a layer of plushness to any sofa, and can be updated easily when you feel it's time for a change. (Look for pillow covers with zippers, buttons, or ties for easy removal and cleaning.)

THE TUFTED OTTOMAN ADDS ANOTHER SPLASH OF COLOR, AND PROVIDES A COMFY RESTING PLACE FOR WEARY FEET.

Find a Quiet Corner

Doesn't everyone yearn at times for a cozy spot to curl up with a good book or perhaps doze off for a catnap? With the active lifestyle of today's families, it's especially important that the living space offers an area for a little quiet time (or time-out, depending on the family member!). Some living room layouts include a nook that can be transformed easily into a quiet relaxation zone. In others, a neglected corner may become a favorite sitting spot simply by adding an overstuffed armchair. It may not require much space to add a window seat, a wonderful way to take advantage of the light streaming into your room. Even if the layout of your living room doesn't lend itself naturally to a quiet spot, the essential elements of the cozy corner can be retrofitted to any space—all you need is a comfortable place to sit, a perch to rest a book or a cup of tea, the right lighting, and a peaceful moment away from the demands of the day.

RIGHT: This charming alcove has been designed to take full advantage of the light-filled space. Tall windows on two sides let in plenty of natural light. A pair of petite armchairs allows for intimate conversations. The chairs are upholstered in an ivory fabric that can stand up to the sun's rays (darker fabrics would quickly fade), as can the pale floral rug.

A RADIATOR COVER TURNS AN OTHERWISE UNUSED SURFACE INTO A CONVENIENT PLACE TO STACK OVERSIZED BOOKS.

OPPOSITE: Old-fashioned details can add character to new construction. Here, wainscoting beneath the windows lends a nostalgic touch to this sunny space. It visually supports the shelf that runs along the base of the windows and provides a useful surface for displaying plants and other objects. It also shields the reading pile that seems to grow next to any comfy chair.

LEFT: Clear away the clutter to transform a corner of your living room into a tranquil spot. Choose seating that encourages relaxation, such as this antique chaise, which brings the comforts of the bedroom right into the living room. In this room, soft wall colors and pale fabrics have a calming effect. The chaise's exotic dark wood contrasts with its off-white upholstery as well as the smooth carpeting beneath it.

BRING AN OUTDOOR TABLE INDOORS FOR A COUNTRY GARDEN TOUCH.

L E F T : Make the most of the built-in features of your living room. Here, an oversized hearth is the ideal place to situate a comfy chair. With carefully chosen details, an all-white decorative scheme can be cozy—this chair is outfitted with a white cotton slipcover with subtle striped pillows, while a white cable-knit throw provides added comfort. Nestled next to the hearth, this arrangement says "cozy corner."

FINDING NEW PURPOSES FOR OLD THINGS IS A HALLMARK OF COUNTRY DESIGN. THIS VINTAGE METAL TUB MAKES AN UNUSUAL BUT EFFECTIVE FIREWOOD CONTAINER.

Make a Quick Change

Turn an antique bench into a side table. Old workbenches can be found in various sizes, and are becoming increasingly collectible. If one is not tall enough to do the job, then try stacking two or more on top of each other. Keep an eye out for other items that might serve as small tables—vintage picnic baskets, boxes, and trunks will also do the job.

LEFT: A small alcove with a single window offers the perfect place to tuck a comfy chair. Although the main part of the room is in view, this arrangement creates a sense of separateness. An assortment of collections on display adds country charm.

ABOVE: A traditionally styled living room features a wingchair in a classic blue that provides a comfortable place to read and reflect. An antique bench is tucked alongside to ensure a place to rest a favorite magazine or a snack. The antique carpet defines the area, picking up the blue used throughout the room.

Gather Around

Whether you like to host intimate gatherings or stage festive get-togethers for larger groups, you'll want a living space that allows you to gather family and friends comfortably. A little bit of forethought makes it simple to transform a non-friendly room into one that is inviting and accommodating. The key is to figure out your entertaining style, then create the right conditions for the gatherings you want to have. Consider practical matters: seating, surfaces, refreshments, and movement. Think about ways to incorporate additional seating into the room for those times when you need to accommodate more guests.

RIGHT: Moving furniture away from the walls and toward the center of a room helps create an environment that encourages people to interact—it literally brings them together. Place tables strategically so they provide convenient surfaces for refreshments but don't obstruct movement. And when it's just your own family, why not gather around your favorite board game for a fun-filled evening? A sisal rug defines this conversation area where classic club chairs are arranged in a cozy circle. A small coffee table provides the perfect resting-place for a glass of wine, and can be easily moved out of the way to create more space.

KILIM PILLOWS WITH FLAME-STITCH PATTERNS AND A RICHLY HUED PAISLEY THROW ADD WARMTH.

Make a Quick Change

Display pictures as a collection
for a dramatic effect. In this room,
four related pictures are presented as
a series. Depending on the space
that you have to fill, experiment with
arranging pictures in rows, diagonally,
or in a checkerboard pattern.

ABOVE: Ample seating is arranged to maximize
interaction in this living room that blends modern and
traditional styles. Four matching upholstered chairs
with simple silhouettes can be moved toward the center of this room for guests. The neutral fabric chosen
for the chairs blends harmoniously with the subtle colors used throughout the room. A soothing green was
selected for the walls, decorative details are
restrained, and unadorned windows feature simple
shades in a natural material. The sofa adds textural
interest while the neutral rug unobtrusively anchors
the space. An arrangement like this is ideal when a
small group gathers.

A B O V E : Transforming a country cupboard into a
bar is an excellent way to turn your living room into a
more functional entertaining space. Bottles are organized in an antique trough, which keeps things tidy
while also serving to protect the surface of the cupboard. There's just enough room for a bowl of lemons
and limes to complete this self-service country bar.

RIGHT: Few pleasures surpass that of gathering around an open fire. This elegant living space takes full advantage of the generous fireplace by positioning the sofa in full view of the dancing flames. Two chairs with curvy lines are drawn close on either side, while a tufted ottoman serves as an impromptu coffee table—a large circular tray transforms the upholstered ottoman into a more useful surface for drinks and a delicate stem or two.

A TEMPORARY BAR CAN BE SET UP OUT OF THE WAY SO THAT REFRESHMENTS ARE EASILY ACCESSIBLE.

Get Media Savvy

Many living rooms today do double duty as entertainment centers, homework areas, and even home offices. With a multipurpose space comes the need to contain all the electronics that have found their way into our daily lives—and cleaning up the media clutter will refresh the room dramatically. The best media storage solutions provide easy access and protection, while organizing items large and small. The many styles of entertainment cabinets available today complement different decors. Or, if you're looking for a project, why not convert an antique wardrobe into a media cabinet? (Remember to cut holes in the back for power cords and to ensure adequate ventilation.) To tackle your media storage needs, first take stock of all your electronics—everything from computers to DVDs—then consider whether a freestanding or built-in solution will work best in your room. Space and budget are two other considerations you'll want to keep in mind.

RIGHT: The generous proportions and high ceiling of this living room allow for an oversized antique armoire that has been converted into a media center. It holds the television, VCR, and DVD player with storage for tapes and disks below. (Its interior shelves were reinforced to accommodate the heavy equipment.) The best part about confining all your electronics to one cabinet is that they can be hidden behind closed doors when not in use.

LEFT: Careful planning yields a tidy wall that includes stacked media cabinets with open storage for firewood below. Painting the cabinets white offsets them from the surrounding tile while linking them with the trim found throughout the room—a smart way to ensure a unified look.

ABOVE: The lack of wall space in this living room presented a challenge. The solution? Moving the sofa away from the wall, adding a wall-mounted IV, and bringing in a freestanding console that packs a lot of storage into a compact unit. The open shelves, flanked by glass-front cabinets, keep multiple electronics accessible.

THE WOOD USED FOR THE MEDIA
CABINET MATCHES THE WOOD
USED THROUGHOUT THE ROOM,
WHILE A SMALL NICHE ABOVE
THE CABINET ADDS AN
ARCHITECTURAL ELEMENT AND
PROVIDES MORE SPACE.

ABOVE: Oversized windows with wonderful views
provide great light and visual stimulation, but not
much wall space for shelves. The answer? Moving the
furnishings to the center of this open living room and
adding built-in storage. The modern hearth incorpo-
rates an adjacent media center, which means that
when this family gathers, whether they want to relax
around the open fire for a quiet evening or watch a
movie, all the necessary equipment is readily available.

A B O V E : A flea market find has been transformed into a media cabinet while preserving its country style. The distressed finish of the cupboard is right at home among the salvaged architectural elements featured throughout the room, yet it's been outfitted with new shelving and ventilation holes.

Define Your Space

One of the joys of open-plan designs is the easy flow from one area to the other. Yet when one room has to serve more than one purpose, it becomes important to designate distinct areas for different activities. Great rooms—rooms that combine living, kitchen, and dining areas in one large space—can be divided in any number of ways. Look to existing architectural elements, decorative details, or strategic placement of furnishings to define the space. If you're thinking about knocking down walls in your home or are in the planning stages for a new home, consider how an open space might be arranged into zones that correspond with the way your family works and plays.

RIGHT: An open-plan great room with a vaulted ceiling enjoys a sense of openness, with exposed Douglas fir beams frame the room and a warm wood floor. The arrangement of the comfortable upholstered pieces, clustered around the ceramic-tiled fireplace, creates a cozy gathering area within the openness.

AN AREA RUG DEFINES THE LIVING SPACE, ANCHORING THE SEATING AROUND THE HEARTH.

Make a Quick Change

Keep things light and airy with white curtains or sheers, then add a splash of color with a border. Pick a color found elsewhere in the room or use fabric that's featured on pillows or furnishings. The border on these curtains looks as if it's been cut with giant pinking shears. If you want to try this on your own, create a stencil to follow or chalk the fabric before cutting.

ABOVE: Rustic elements—like the antique farm table—set the tone for this room, while the collection of terracotta pots on the mantel adds an earthy touch. Placing the sofa directly in front of the country hearth, with Its back towards the dining table, serves to separate the two areas. The brick floor, laid in a herringbone pattern, provides unifying texture throughout the room, but the throw rugs serve to warm up the living area, and visually separate it from the dining area.

LEFT: The opening between the living and dining areas of this home was enlarged to improve the flow from one space to the next. Traffic now flows freely from the kitchen right through to the living area, and the hearth can be enjoyed from both the living and dining spaces.

A PAIR OF MATCHING AREA RUGS DEFINES THE LIVING AND DINING AREAS, WHILE TILE FLOORING UNIFIES THE TWO SPACES.

Embrace Nature

A view of nature is uplifting even when enjoyed at a distance…and from the comfort of your own home. Incorporating nature's beauty is an essential part of country style. Bring the outdoors into your living room by making the most of your views—whether your windows offer an awe-inspiring natural landscape, a glimpse of green from your garden, or even just a patch of blue from an apartment skylight. Well-placed windows and glass doors are the most obvious way to take advantage of surrounding natural beauty. When building a new home, take note of your exposures and plan accordingly. Adding windows to an existing home will require the help of a professional, yet is a wonderful way to bring new life to any space. Depending upon where you live, you may even be able to extending your living space with an outdoor room, patio, or balcony.

RIGHT: The uninterrupted view from this open dining/living room extends as far as the eye can see. Full-length windows frame the expansive view, while letting in light and fresh air. Above, a small, square window takes advantage of the vaulted ceiling, and adds architectural interest. The pale hue chosen for the walls and ceiling enhances the light and airy feel of the room.

ABOVE: A modern fireplace is surrounded by storage that makes good use of the space yet allows for even more windows. The view becomes almost panoramic. Note the open shelves just below the counter and in the corner, offering convenient display space.

RIGHT: Enlarging the doorway between the living room and a sunny alcove ensures that the views can be enjoyed from both spaces, while maximizing the available light. The greenery outside serves as a lush backdrop for the minimal space while the coffee-table garden brings the outdoors inside.

Bringing Outdoor Plants In

● Create a container garden for an outdoor patio or terrace that can be spirited indoors before the first frost. In regions with cold winters, this is a way to enjoy tender ornamentals—like citrus, Japanese camellias, and palms—all year long.

● Prepare pots of spring bulbs in the autumn so that you'll have seasonal color indoors—daffodils, tulips, and narcissus are a few good choices.

● In the full bloom of summer, create indoor window boxes filled with summery flowers or herbs.

● Consider native species when planning an indoor "garden." Creating a look that mirrors the natural landscape is a sure way to blur the boundary between indoors and out.

LEFT: If you live in a climate that is suited to outdoor entertaining, consider opening your living room directly to the outdoors. A small stone or brick patio is all that's needed to create a level space for a dining table and chairs. French doors that open to the outside are an attractive solution that allows you to move easily between indoors and out.

ABOVE: The centerpiece of this crisp white living room actually lies outside the home—in the view of the water just beyond the glass doors. Sliding doors maximize the view, while mullions create the effect of paned windows. The simplicity of the furnishings and white palette combine for a summery look that is cool and refreshing, while not competing with the view.

LEFT: Windowed doors, flanked by windows that let in even more light, provide easy access to the outdoors and a clear view of activities in the yard. White-stained oak floors in this modest kitchen/living room enhance the sense of openness, and the pastel hues keep the look lighthearted.

A SIMPLE COUNTRY TOUCH THAT INCREASES NATURE'S PRESENCE IN YOUR HOME IS DECO- RATING WITH FRESH FLOWERS, FRUITS, AND VEGETABLES.

White on White

The simplicity and purity of white makes it a popular approach for modern country spaces…yet white is not quite as simple as it appears. There are many different nuances of white, ranging from cool whites with blue or lavender undertones to warm whites with creamy overtones. The clean, calm qualities of white make it easy to live with and open up a range of decorating possibilities. It's an ideal choice for a small room as it makes every space look larger and reflects natural light. It's also a quick way to refresh a flea market find or transform a brick wall into a textured backdrop. You may decide to whitewash everything from floor to ceiling, and introduce a variety of textures—or add other hues to contrast with your mainly white scheme. Either way, the beauty of white is its versatility, and the way it allows your personal style to shine through.

RIGHT: Nearly everything in this room is white yet it doesn't appear cold. Textures are the key. Wood floors offer a warm contrast to the white area rug, as does the unfinished surface of the coffee table, which sits atop painted white legs. The chunky chairs and sofa are dressed in white slipcovers to bring out a softer, more delicate effect.

FOR A PURE WHITE LOOK, PAINT THE MANTLE AND THE BRICKS AROUND THE FIREPLACE WHITE.

OPPOSITE: Painting furniture white will allow you to combine pieces that otherwise might not exist in the same room harmoniously. In this elegant space, the details of an elaborate full-length mirror are downplayed when its frame is painted white. An Empire table is transformed into soft, curvy forms with a fresh coat of paint. And a petite chaise that recalls another era looks perfectly at home amid the larger pieces. The continuity of the whitewash brings everything together in a soft, appealing unity.

LEFT: White brings out the texture of the delicate scrolls that encircle this mirror.

COUNTRY STYLE INCLUDES GLAMOROUS TOUCHES: AN ELABORATE CRYSTAL CHANDELIER DRAWS THE EYE UPWARD.

R I G H T : Finishes and fabrics add texture and visual interest to an all-white living room. Oversized pillows fashioned from vintage linens feature a nubby pattern that contrasts with the smooth finish of the sofa. A large coffee table is left in its distressed state, adding a rustic element to the room. (You can achieve this look by chipping or scraping the surface of a painted table.)

AN ANTIQUE WICKER TRAY AND WIRE BASKET ADD TEXTURE TO THE TABLETOP.

ABOVE: White tulips grace a painted mantel
and add nature's white tones to the room.

THE SUBTLE PLAID OF THIS WOVEN RUG ADDS
A WARM NOTE TO THIS LIGHT AND AIRY ROOM.

ABOVE: A splash of color in an all-white room is eye-catching and invigorating. Choose colorful accessories for this effect—think pillows, throws, and curtains, or collectibles, such as glassware. Here, an apple-green throw on the slipcovered sofa picks up the tones of the fresh flowers on the table behind, as well as the greenery outside.

Colorful Moods

Working with color is one of the easiest ways to change the mood of any room. It's a good idea to evaluate your living space first—size and shape—before committing to a color scheme. In general, strong wall colors will make a room seem more intimate, while lighter hues will enlarge a space. It's a good idea first to pick a dominant color, then secondary and accent colors. Try colors out before committing to them—start with just one wall. You can give your living space a distinctive look with a fresh coat of paint, but don't confine your colorful thoughts to the walls. Floor coverings, furnishings, and accessories can all get in on the color act, too. A colorful slipcover or the addition of new accessories in a different hue can create a quick transformation for a fresh look or a new season.

R I G H T : A two-toned approach to color turns this country living room into a lively space. The sunflower gold used on the walls is offset by a minty green trim and chair rail. Green also appears on an antique cupboard and the legs of the small coffee table. It's a good rule of thumb to use a color more than once in a room to create a sense of visual unity.

THE PATTERNED RUG ADDS A SPLASH OF COLOR TO THE FLOOR, AND COMPLEMENTS THE BRIGHTLY PAINTED SURFACE OF THE COFFEE TABLE.

A B O V E : While the sofa in this room is a neutral white, the brilliant blue from the rug is picked up in the slipcovered armchair and a nearby floor vase. Slipcovers are a good way to experiment with color as they can be changed easily as the mood strikes.

FRESH GREEN CUSHIONS ADORN
A PAIR OF WICKER CHAIRS AND
MATCH THE TONE OF THE
PAINTINGS HANGING BEHIND.

A B O V E : A bright slipcover and a purple coffee table
are paired for a whimsical effect. Decorative painting
on the wall behind the sofa disguises a closed fireplace while the modern still life above the mantel adds
a splash of color. Art is a great way to add color and
visual interest to any room.

ABOVE: If you select a bold color for the walls, choose secondary and accent colors that are mid-toned or lighter. Here, a country cupboard (with birdhouse on top), mantel, and salvaged architectural details break up the intensity of the wall color, and keep the primary color from becoming too dominant.

RIGHT: To emphasize a strong wall color, use a crisp white on the ceiling and trim. The autumnal orange of this room's walls lends a warm glow. Oversized furnishings feature accessories in the same hue, while a collection of country quilts and pillows enlivens the white sofa.

RIGHT: A traditional country living room gets a mini-makeover when the woodwork is painted green. The mantel and adjacent shelves become a focal point of the room, while the windows—also trimmed in green—become colorful accents around the room. The ceiling beam seems to draw all the brightly hued elements together.

GREEN ACCENTS DOT THE ROOM—NOTE THE FABRICS USED ON UPHOLSTERED PIECES AND THE DECORATIVE PLATES DISPLAYED ABOVE THE FIREPLACE.

Decorating with Color

1. Choose a dominant color first. Consider painting one wall to see how you feel about the primary color, and how it changes throughout the day.

2. Pick secondary and accent colors. You should choose only one secondary color, but you can choose up to two accent colors. To spark some ideas, get a color wheel. Choose complements that are opposites on the color wheel, but opt for shades of these colors for a subtler look. Or you can accent with lighter shades within the same family of colors.

3. Consider how you use a room before committing to colors. Many people like to save bold colors for rooms that aren't used often; use mid-range hues in small spaces; and feature more neutral tones in the rooms that are used most often.

LEFT: An antique hutch might have gone unnoticed if placed directly against the warm-hued wall. Instead, a colorful country quilt serves as a backdrop, and offsets the detail of the beautiful hutch.

ABOVE: An old-fashioned cottage yellow is the perfect backdrop for this collection of American craft pottery, contrasting with the muted shades of the vases, and highlighting their shapes. The bright pink frame adds a colorful country touch.

ABOVE: Colorful fabric that matches the drapes spruces up curvaceous chairs. The table runner adds a splash of color that can easily change with your mood!

RIGHT: This living room defies tradition by opting for a modern color palette with classic furnishings. Traditional stripes adorn a pair of camelback sofas, while back bolsters pick up the chartreuse walls. Lavender drapes provide a calming contrast.

Make a Quick Change

Turn your mantel into a "gallery" in which the art changes regularly. Instead of hanging paintings and photographs permanently on the walls, why not prop them up on the mantel? It strikes a casual note, and pictures can be looked at more closely. Change the display whenever the mood strikes. The mantel is also a good spot for flowers, seasonal decorations, or objets d'art.

On Display

Collections are a mainstay of country style. Displaying collections and favorite objects always adds an appealing personal flair to a room; how to show them off and yet not turn the living room into a showroom is the challenge. If you have not amassed a collection, note that even everyday objects become decorative when placed in full view. When you're looking for ways to add display space to your living room, don't overlook even the smallest nooks and crannies...a cleverly-designed corner cabinet lets you transform an empty corner into valuable storage space, while a shelf situated above a window or door draws the eye upward and keeps precious items away from the fray. Of course, if you have the room, consider turning an entire wall into a showcase. Simple, open shelving can house everything from books to pottery.

R I G H T : A traditional built-in cabinet offers the perfect place to display a delicate collection of antique teapots, cups, and saucers. Glass-fronted cabinets on either side offer more storage for overflow china and books.

THE CRISP WHITE SHELVES, PALE GREEN WALL, AND PINK CHINA MAKE A CHEERFUL STATEMENT.

ABOVE: When you're looking for surfaces to turn into display space, take stock of the architecture of your room. The mantel in this period home becomes a convenient place to showcase a collection of glass vessels and lamps. Think about rotating collections to create seasonal displays in your home.

RIGHT: There are many ways to decorate with collections. Thanks to simple wire plate hangers, a trio of antique plates becomes art. The vintage charm of the outdoor chair and retro pillow complete the installation.

Make a Quick Change

Repurpose an attractive object—
such as this decorative urn—to
stow firewood. The architectural
form of the urn complements the
handsome mantel, and gets the
firewood up off the ground,
making it easier to grasp. Other
outdoor vessels that can be
turned into fireplace accessories
include vintage milk crates,
wooden boxes, harvest baskets,
and buckets of all kinds.

ARRANGE OBJECTS
OF VARIOUS SHAPES
AND SIZES WITH AN
EYE TOWARD CREAT-
ING AN INTERESTING
VISUAL DISPLAY.

LEFT: Floor-to-ceiling shelves transform a shallow recess, adjacent to the hearth, into a space to display the owner's collection of African art and artifacts. When objects within a theme are displayed as a single collection, the overall effect can be more dramatic than when shown individually.

ABOVE: Traditional corner cabinets have been solving storage needs for years. A glass-fronted cabinet above allows contents to be enjoyed whether doors are open or not. Closed storage below provides a place to stow items that aren't suitable for display.

The Slipcovered Look

Originally, slipcovers were employed as a way to protect furniture. Times have changed and now they are practically a hallmark of the new country style. Slipcovers range from neatly tailored styles that mimic upholstered tailoring to loose and flowing styles with ties or buttons that have a more casual look. Whether you're drawn to the slipcovered look in itself, or because you need to mask a worn-out chair, or you simply want to update your sofa, you'll find a variety of slipcovers to meet your needs.

Slipcovers can be found (or sewn) for just about any type of seating. And the practical benefits of slipcovers—most are wash-and-wear—make them particularly attractive for families with children. A simple way to give your living space a quick makeover is to change slipcovers with the seasons—crisp white cotton or natural linen for summer can be replaced with a cozy corduroy or chenille slipcover for the winter months. For a refined look, add elegant lighting and accessories.

RIGHT: Cotton slipcovers have an old-world elegance when paired with beautiful hardwood floors and a few selected antiques. Fine linens drape the tables for a soft, all-white look. The painting behind the sofa provides a self-portrait of sorts—offering a glimpse of a room within a room—while the sofa's deep cushions provide real comfort.

L E F T : A chunky chair is slimmed by a tailored slipcover with neat piping at the seams.

A B O V E : In this room, a boxy slipcover drapes one chair while the other is neatly upholstered. Within the room's off-white palette, the different two chairs work as a pair.

ACCESSORIZE THE SLIPCOVERED LOOK
WITH ANTIQUES AND OTHER SALVAGED
ITEMS—AN ANTIQUE DOOR IS TRANS-
FORMED INTO A PEDESTAL.

LEFT: While not exactly a slipcover, this antique chair features cushions with buttons down the center that make it look like the checkered fabric can be changed as quickly as a shirt. The tailored look transforms the elegant antique into an everyday chair with a bit of whimsy.

ABOVE: Slipcovered seating is the ideal choice for this rustic living room. Appointed with unfinished antiques and salvaged architectural finds, the rough surfaces are softened by linen slipcovers that lighten the mood.

L E F T : When a piece of furniture is past its prime, look to a slipcover that provides complete coverage to effect your transformation. This slipcover drapes the sofa in a casual fashion and has a wavy bottom that brushes the floor. The hardwood floors, rocker, and side chair balance the unstructured look of the slip-covered sofa, while decorative details are purposefully unfussy.

A SLIPCOVER EFFECT ON THE ROCKING CHAIR ADDS A TOUCH OF WHIMSY AS WELL AS COMFORT, AND LINKS THE CHAIR AND SOFA VISUALLY.

Mix New and Old

The love of old things is at the core of country style, yet today's most successful expressions of it have an eye to both the past and present. Antiques and collected objects live in eclectic harmony with reproductions and modern touches that offer greater functionality. While you pay tribute to pieces that have been preserved from one generation to the next, think about the needs of your family today. You may opt for new furnishings that offer the ultimate in comfort and have the durability to stand up to everyday use, while antique accessories add a note from the past. There is no right or wrong when it comes to country style. After all, traditions are deeply personal and established over time.

RIGHT: One way to update a traditional chair is with new fabric. Here, classic wingback chairs are given a new look with crisp cotton slipcovers in white. The chairs are paired with an antique daybed that's been converted into a sofa and covered in traditional checkered fabric. Other antique details around the room include a chest that's been turned into a coffee table and an antique barrel that keeps magazines and newspapers organized by the chair.

LEFT: A collection of country objects from various sources creates a visually appealing display. Atop an antique cupboard, Shaker–style wood boxes and an early pitcher are in the foreground, while antique board games serve as the backdrop.

ABOVE: The star motif is a country favorite. Here it is repeated throughout this room in a variety of ways—an antique Chinese checkers board hangs on the wall, a bookend features both a star and a sliver of the moon, and the star that rests atop the occasional table is a lantern.

RIGHT: The original details of this home are softened by a coat of paint on the woodwork—everything from the ceiling beams to the steps—in a warm yellow shade. A light rug defines the sitting area, and also helps to brighten the space, while a smaller quilt-inspired rug is layered on top—adding a bit of color beneath the checkered demi-sofa.

A LADDERBACK CHAIR WITH WOVEN SEAT IS PAIRED WITH AN INTRICATELY CARVED ROCKER—AS YOU FIND PIECES THAT YOU LIKE, MIX AND MATCH THEM FOR CASUAL, CLASSIC COUNTRY CHARM.

RIGHT: Portraits displayed on the mantel pay tribute to family ancestors yet co-exist with modern elements such as the floor lamp, a pair of ottoman cubes, and the updated club chair.

OPPOSITE: Combining new and old pieces is one way to ensure that your living room meets the demands of your lifestyle, while enjoying a traditional look. Two contemporary overstuffed sofas are designed for comfort, while antiques throughout the room add a nostalgic note—stacked wooden stools serve as an end table and a long workbench holds books behind the sofa.

CHECKERBOARD IS SO VERSATILE—IT WORKS WITH BOTH A CONTEMPORARY STRIPED PILLOW AND AN ANTIQUE QUILT GRACING THE OTTOMAN.

A SALVAGED SIGN
BECOMES A FOCAL
POINT WHEN PLACED
ON THE MANTEL.
THE EQUESTRIAN
THEME REAPPEARS
IN THE ANTIQUE
HORSE PLACED BY
THE WINDOW.

Make a Quick Change

Opt for curtains with tabs so that you can show off a decorative rod that picks up the style of your living room. There's been an explosion of options in curtain rods from wrought iron to bamboo, and they can be paired with a wide assortment of finials. Why not mix and match two different finials on one rod? For a colorful statement, choose an unfinished wood rod and paint it whatever color suits your mood. New curtains will complete the transformation.

L E F T : A handsome living room strikes the perfect balance between modern and traditional style: The black and white rug adds a strong graphic element to the room yet recalls a traditional checkerboard motif. A pair of coffee tables features woven surfaces inspired by traditional seating, while the upholstered furnishings are strictly modern with streamlined silhouettes and neutral fabrics.

Modern Country Living

Clean, simple, architectural—the qualities that make modern design appealing also make it a good match for many treasured country pieces. Country elements can add texture and visual interest, and transform a sterile living room into a warm and personal one. Similarly, vintage architecture can seem quite modern when emphasized by paint (or stripped of it) or when paired with modern furnishings. Try combining different materials in unexpected ways: rustic and sleek, natural and man-made. Match leather furnishings with soft chenille throws. Leave beams exposed as a counterpoint to smooth flooring. Or display antiques and artifacts that introduce a rustic element to a modern space. One way to create a living room that feels modern is to start with furniture that has clean, smooth lines, then warm it up with fabric, accessories, color, or collectibles.

R I G H T : The small proportions of this living room are well suited to its sleekly modern style. The curvilinear bench becomes a focal point of the room, and its backless style allows light from the French doors to pass through it. The colors used throughout the room are subtle and soothing.

A PAIR OF FLOOR LAMPS ARCHES OVER EITHER END OF THE BENCH FOR AN UNDERSTATED YET ARCHITECTURAL LIGHTING SOLUTION.

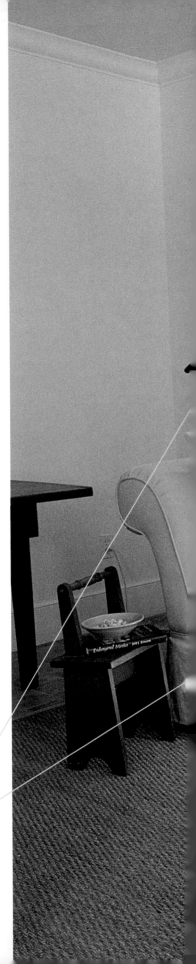

ABOVE: What this room lacks in space, it more than makes up for in style, beginning with the entryway. A pair of smooth classical columns frames the doorway and helps to distinguish the living room from the entryway. Their symmetry is repeated in other pairings in the room.

RIGHT: Comfort is not sacrificed for style in this sophisticated country house. The look is decidedly modern, including the minimal hearth and art hanging above, yet the space is warm and inviting. The neutral palette used throughout the room creates a harmonious effect that is restful and calming.

NOTE THE CLEVER STORAGE—BUILT-IN
SHELVES AROUND THE DOORWAY TAKE
UP NO EXTRA ROOM AND OFFER AN
IDEAL PLACE TO STASH BOOKS.

Make a Quick Change

Layer rugs on top of each other to create a special comfort zone. When your feet touch the ground (or not!) they're greeted with an extra layer of comfort. This room features a natural woven runner—in a darker hue than the primary floor covering—that sits directly in front of the leather daybed. Place a patterned rug over a solid one to define space or add visual interest to the room—a layered effect can help focus attention where you want it.

AN ABSTRACT PAINTING DOMINATES ONE WALL AND IS FLANKED BY A PAIR OF MIRRORS THAT ECHO ITS GEOMETRIC SHAPE.

LEFT : While the main area of the room is designed for socializing, this corner of the living space is strictly for rest and relaxation. A cushioned leather daybed offers a comfortable place for a nap, while the arm-chair can be drawn up to the hearth to enjoy the open flame. A simple beam serves as mantel, and features a trio of modern paintings.

ABOVE : Past and present co-exist in this home in a celebration of modern country style. The wooden ceiling beams are answered by the wide floorboards finished in a natural tone. The black leather seating is a definite modern touch, yet is warmed by plenty of pillows and casual throws.

Eclectic Charm

Some of the most charming living spaces defy easy categorization. Have you ever walked into a room, and wondered if it were traditional or modern? Formal or casual? Chances are, it's a bit of both, created by someone with a strong sense of personal style and a keen eye. An eclectic look is best achieved by following your own instincts, and drawing from various sources. Mix a flea market side chair with a modern sofa that offers genuine comfort. Display treasures collected during your travels. Or re-purpose an object to create the effect of a room that's come into being over time. One of the best parts of an eclectic look is that you can get started with whatever you have on hand. Check the attic for an antique mirror or wrought-iron sconce that can be dusted off. The ideal living space should reflect who you are and your personal style—and chances are that's an eclectic mix!

RIGHT: The faded elegance of this living room is achieved with a mix of classic furnishings, salvaged architectural finds, and elegant accessories that recall another era. The gilded mirror that hangs behind the sofa is a focal point, and is flanked by dressy sconces that drip crystals, while columns on either side frame the elegant tableau.

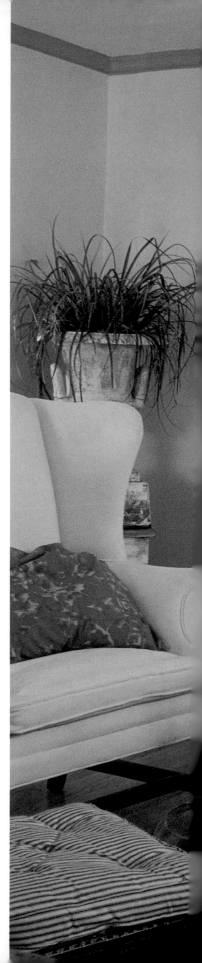

LEFT: A collection of antique spheres becomes an interesting display atop an old table. A mirror with just the right patina reflects the orbs.

ABOVE: This is a room that truly reflects the passions of Its owners. Large hand-painted panels adorn two walls with antique sconces mounted directly to them. The placement of the furnishings also reflects an unconventional eye. In many rooms, the statue atop the pedestal might be a focal point...here, it is just one of the interesting objects that contribute to the eclectic style.

OPPOSITE: Displaying personal collections is one way to ensure that a room reflects your individuality. What makes this sunny living space special is the objets d'art that are interspersed throughout the room— candelabras, urns, statuary, and vintage mirrors create a charmingly cluttered effect. Along with the many mirrors, a pair of crystal chandeliers captures and reflects the abundant natural light in the room.

LEFT: Note the clever placement of a salvaged window nestled between two real ones, and the two slender columns flanking the large mirror. Don't be afraid to layer objects with different forms and textures to create a truly original display.

PLANTS AND FLOWERS ADD LIFE TO ANY ROOM.

A B O V E : A warm palette unifies this otherwise varied room: A crystal chandelier dangles high above, while a glass table with an elaborate metal base takes center stage below. Leopard print enlivens a pair of regal chairs, while unadorned sofas slipcovered in white provide everyday comfort.

R I G H T : Develop a theme through placement and a shared color palette. A still life featuring flowers in reds and oranges rests against an antique mantel, which is illuminated by the soft glow of the ceramic lamp with a single tulip gracing its base. A circular pillow in the same tones adorns the nearby chair.

Make a Quick Change

SELECT A CORNER TO CREATE A VIGNETTE OF FAVORITE ITEMS— HERE, A GILDED MIR- ROR IS THE BACK- DROP FOR A FULL-SIZE BUST, STATUESQUE LAMP, AND OTHER CHERISHED OBJECTS.

Turn to salvaged architectural finds to add an eclectic touch to your room. Windows can be hung on walls as is or the glass can be replaced with mirrors. An antique mantel can be used to create a faux fireplace or simply be displayed for its intricate design. Columns and other architectural details (like newel posts and finials) also make interesting appointments.

LEFT: A 19th-century burled-wood cabinet that was once used to store food and cooking implements in a Japanese kitchen is turned into a storage center that becomes a focal point of the living room. The dark wood cabinet is offset by the whitewashed floors, which feature a richly textured rug.

ABOVE: Sky-blue walls serve as an airy backdrop for family heirlooms. An inherited down-filled sofa has been updated in a buttery damask; a large drum is called upon as an end table; and the low-slung coffee table was brought back from Morocco at the beginning of the 20th century.

Storage Made Simple

Transform your living room by eliminating unnecessary clutter with efficient storage—it can be done without sacrificing style or space. Shelves and cabinets are the basic storage ingredients, but add baskets, bins, and boxes to expand your options. If you are working with an irregular space or trying to turn a quirky area into a storage center, it may be best to opt for a custom storage unit. Think about the types of items you need to stow so you can design a storage plan that suits your needs. If you're a book-lover, an expanse of open shelving can turn your living room into a library. If it's a music collection that needs to be stored, perhaps you'll want a drawer unit that hides CDs while keeping them accessible. Or consider a cabinet that offers both open and hidden storage, if you'd like to display a few treasured items while keeping others out of view.

R I G H T : Large baskets fit below a well-worn farm table, providing discreet storage for an extensive quilt collection. When collections are kept on hand, they can be easily rotated into the room's display—here a circa-1910 white-on-red Flying Geese variation takes a turn on the far wall.

RUSTIC SHELVES OFFER
MORE DISPLAY SPACE.

ABOVE: The antique table and well-loved collections give this city apartment the feeling of a country home. The open-weave baskets are an ideal storage solution to keep quilts visible but out of the way.

RIGHT: For this family of book-lovers, the shelves are integrated into the design of the room, while providing ample storage for books and other objects. Shelves with no back means that the red wall remains visible, unifying the room's color scheme, while the white matches the woodwork throughout.

Shelving Tips

1. Think in terms of linear footage when calculating your shelving needs. A single 6-foot long shelf offers six linear feet of storage—a unit with 6 such shelves offers 36 linear feet.

2. For a rough idea of the shelving you require, measure the linear footage of whatever you plan to store—books, tapes, etc.—then allow extra space for open display.

3. Shelf depth and height will also be determined by the objects that you plan to store. Add an inch or two of "head space" above the objects for easy access.

4. Place regularly used items from eye level to waist height, with less-used items occupying the highest and lowest shelves.

LEFT: Oversized coffee table books, a pleasure to look at, are often difficult to shelve. This shallow recess just left of the hearth is fitted with special shelves designed to hold just such a collection. The individual shelves were built low deliberately so that the art books could be arranged in stacks.

ABOVE: Instead of extending all the way to the ceiling, shelves stop three-quarters of the way up, creating a convenient surface for display. The oil paintings set casually on top of the shelves share a common theme: the cottage rose.

Make a Quick Change

When you're out of shelf space, hang family photos on the wall as you would any treasured piece of art. It's a good way to make sure precious photos remain in good condition. There is a plethora of frames and mat materials to choose from. The series of photos here features simple white mats yet they are mounted off center, which draws the eye toward the image.

FEEL FREE TO STACK A GROUP OF PAINTINGS OR PHOTOGRAPHS; THIS DISPLAY INVITES CLOSER INSPECTION.

L E F T : A simple set of shelves transforms the space between the window and the wall into an efficient storage center. When built-in bookshelves are not an option, there are many "off the shelf" varieties. The slim shelving used here blends in with many of the white elements of the room, and preserves the light and airy feel.

A B O V E : The built-in storage cabinet in this living room features the same decorative wood moldings as the wall behind it. Although added at a later date, they look as if they were part of the original design. The unit is deeper than a typical cabinet, and the copious surface becomes a display area for a collection of oil paintings and antique frames.

Cottage Appeal

The appeal of the country cottage is timeless—and the cottage look need not be limited to homes in country locales. You can recreate the charm of an English country cottage no matter where you live. For the basics of the cottage look, think floral fabrics, painted furniture, and collectibles on display. For a quick transformation, you might want to outfit your sofa with a slipcover in a floral print, give a pine table or cupboard a coat of pastel paint, or accent the room with antique china. For a more profound change, you may want to reupholster furniture in a mix of florals and patterns, and display one or more collections. You can embrace cottage style wholeheartedly or embellish your room with just a few cheerful details—it's a versatile look.

RIGHT: This cozy sitting room seems a perfect spot for an afternoon tea party. Pale green walls set the tone, while white woodwork highlights the architectural details of the room. Comfortable chairs are slipcovered in different floral prints that all work together. When mixing patterns and prints, choose colors that are within the same family or shade.

BASKETS ARE CASUALLY NESTED, AND TURNED INTO AN IMPROMPTU TABLE WHEN IT'S TIME TO SERVE THE TEA.

A B O V E : This living room packs a lot into a small space. A simple bench beneath the window is the perfect perch for perusing a book. A corner cabinet provides convenient storage, while the mantel acts as a display space for antique china and other delicate collectibles.

R I G H T : Pretty in pink is the theme of this cheerful country cottage. Floral, striped, and toile fabrics are mixed and matched to charming effect. The ruffled skirt on the chair and ottoman add a dressy feel, while unfussy window treatments allow the sunlight to stream in unfiltered.

Make a Quick Change

Transform an exposed radiator into a useful surface with a slab of marble, slate, or granite (ceramic tiles left over from the kitchen or bath will also do the trick). It's a simple way to turn an otherwise unusable space into a convenient display surface. Radiator cabinets that cover the entire unit are best if the radiator is in use.

RIGHT: A more formal country cottage features an elegant living room bathed in golden hues. Instead of country florals, silk damask was selected for the sofa, which features a billowy skirt in the same fabric. When opened, a built-in cupboard reveals a collection of china that can be accessed easily.

THE DECORATIVE DETAILS ON THE FACE OF THE MANTEL ARE PAINTED GOLD TO REFLECT THE WARM TONES OF THE ROOM.

ABOVE: A collection of "cottages" reflects the passion of the homeowners and forms an interesting display in their living room. Weathered furnishings—including a park bench—contribute to the rustic cottage feel, while a comfy sofa and chair that sport crisp white slipcovers offer some contrast. The tranquil landscape paintings seem to expand the view in all directions.

RIGHT: A lofty summer cottage can handle a cluttered collection of stuff. Shelves climb the bare walls, and hold everything from books to electronics, while an oversized mirror dominates the space behind the sofa. Casual slipcovers (with ruffles and ties) and pillows in vintage fabric create an invitingly casual environment perfect for hanging out with friends and family.

ABOVE: A summer cottage features a sun-filled living room that combines indoor and outdoor furnishings in a delightfully fresh way. An Adirondack-style rocker is moved indoors from the porch, while a metal windmill originally from a farm becomes an indoor sculpture.

A RETRO-STYLE COFFEE TABLE WORKS WITHIN THE CLEAN COTTAGE FEEL.

A B O V E : A floral display brings nature's art into the home, as in this trio of glass vessels holding pretty blooms.

The Focal Point

Every room should have a focal point, that is, one element to which all eyes are drawn. Adding or changing the focal point will have a transformative effect. What kind of focal point suits your style? Is it a fabulous antique sofa? An intricate mantel? An astonishing view? A vintage bar trolley? Or a spectacular piece of art? Design your room with the focal point in mind. You may want to arrange seating so that the focus is squarely on this feature, or you might want to position furnishings in a way that balances the room. If you're not sure what to make the focus of your room, think about the one piece without which the room wouldn't be the same. That's your focal point!

RIGHT: A Gustavian sofa evokes Scandinavian country style, and sets the tone for this space. Blue and white checkered fabric draws attention to the delicate form of the piece, and ensures that it is the centerpiece of the room. The oval portrait hung directly above the sofa draws the eye upward, while natural swags of greenery frame the painting and unify the disparate elements.

OTHER HALLMARKS OF SCANDINAVIAN COUNTRY STYLE INCLUDE THE BLEACHED HARD-WOOD FLOORS AND PAINTED FURNISHINGS.

LEFT: Consider the relationship between furnishings and art when deciding on the placement of pieces in your living room. A large oil painting makes a strong statement and adds a sense of drama while the large antique chest serves as a base for the painting.

ABOVE: To offset the dark tones of the oil painting, the room is painted a pale green, along with white for the space above the picture rail and for the trim. A large area rug in a neutral tone draws all the elements of the room together.

ABOVE: Leave some space around important pieces of furniture so that they aren't lost among the rest of the furnishings. Here, an Empire-style sofa is set away from the wall in order to take center stage. Its curvy design can be fully appreciated without the distraction of nearby pieces.

RIGHT: A minimal landscape painting dominates the wall in this cheerful country space. It takes the place of color on the wall, and introduces imagery that sets the tone for the room. The quilt-inspired fabric covering the nearby chair and ottoman seem right at home in the simple farmhouse featured in the painting.

Make a Quick Change

Get inspired by vintage fabrics. Whether you use an antique quilt to cover a chair or create pillows with remnant pieces of fabric, a vintage touch can be easily incorporated. If you're lucky, you'll find vintage fabric in peak condition. Otherwise, look for reproductions that are inspired by vintage designs.

LEFT: A rustic retreat features log walls, rough beams, and a stone hearth that is the literal and social center of this home. A small landscape painting is propped on the mantel, adding a splash of color, with primitive sconces on either side.

ABOVE: Take advantage of your room's most desirable features and plan around them. A traditional hearth is at the center of this cozy gathering spot, and seating is arranged to enjoy the warmth of the fire. Elegant woodwork creates a more formal feeling and complements the built-in cabinetry.

LEFT: Originally, this living room did not have a fireplace. The owners fell in love with the late 19th century mantel at a flea market, and decided to create a hearth that would become the focal point of the room. For a less expensive option, install a mantel decoratively—all you need is the wall space.

EMBELLISHMENTS DRAW THE EYE TO THE HEARTH.

Index

Photo Credits

Country Living would like to thank the many photographers whose work appears on these pages.

Jacket
Front jacket—©Michael Luppino; Back jacket (top left)—©Michael Luppino; Back jacket (top right)—©Michael Luppino; Back jacket (bottom)—©Michael Luppino; Spine—©Keith Scott Morton

Page 1—©Steven Randazzo; Page 2—©Helen Norman; Page 3—©Michael Luppino; Page 5 (top)—©Keith Scott Morton; Page 5 (middle)—©Grey Crawford; Page 5 (bottom)—Courtesy Gridley and Graves

Foreword
Page 7—©Keith Scott Morton

Introduction
Page 9—©Michael Luppino

Country Comfort
Pages 10-11—©Keith Scott Morton; Page 12—©Keith Scott Morton; Page 13—©Keith Scott Morton; Page 14—©Jim Bastardo; Page 15—©Jim Bastardo; Page 16—Courtesy Gridley and Graves; Page 17—©Keith Scott Morton; Page 18—©Keith Scott Morton; Page 19—©Keith Scott Morton

Find a Quiet Corner
Pages 20-21—©Michael Luppino; Page 22—©Michael Luppino; Page 23—©Charles Maraia; Pages 25-26—©Steven Randazzo; Page 26—©Steven Randazzo; Page 27—©Paul Wicheloe

Gather Around
Pages 28-29—©Keith Scott Morton; Page 30—©Keith Scott Morton; Page 31—©Paul Margonelli; Pages 32-33—©Michael Luppino

Get Media Savvy
Pages 34-35—©Keith Scott Morton; Page 36—©Keith Scott Morton; Page 37—©William P. Steele; Page 38—©Keith Scott Morton; Page 39—

Courtesy Gridley and Graves

Define Your Space
Pages 40-41—©Keith Scott Morton; Page 42—©Keith Scott Morton; Page 43—©Steven Randazzo; Pages 44-45—©Keith Scott Morton

Embrace Nature
Pages 46-47—©William P. Steele; Page 48—©William P. Steele; Page 49—©Keith Scott Morton; Page 50—©Keith Scott Morton, photo appears courtesy Cynthia Steffe; Page 51—©Keith Scott Morton; Pages 52-53—©Keith Scott Morton

White on White
Pages 54-55—©Ray Kachatorian; Page 56—©Keith Scott Morton; Page 57—©Keith Scott Morton; Pages 58-59—©Steven Randazzo; Page 60—©Keith Scott Morton; Page 61—©Keith Scott Morton

Colorful Moods
Pages 62-63—©Keith Scott Morton; Page 64—©Keith Scott Morton; Page 65—©Keith Scott Morton; Page 66—©Jessie Walker; Page 67—©Jessie Walker; Pages 68-69—©Keith Scott Morton; Page 70—©Jessie Walker; Page 71—Courtesy Gridley and Graves; Page 72—©Keith Scott Morton; Page 73—©Keith Scott Morton

On Display
Pages 74-75—Courtesy Gridley and Graves; Page 76—©Charles Maraia; Page 77—©Charles Maraia; Page 78—©Keith Scott Morton; Page 79—©Michael Luppino; Pages 80-81—©Michael Luppino; Page 82—©Michael Luppino; Page 83—©Steve Gross and Sue Daley; Page 84—©Steve Gross and Sue Daley; Page 85—©Keith Scott Morton; Pages 86-87—©Keith Scott Morton

The Slipcovered Look
Pages 88-89—©Steve Gross and Sue Daley; Page 90—©Steve Gross and Sue Daley; Page 91—©Steve Gross and Sue Daley; Pages 92-93—©Steve Gross and Sue Daley; Page 94—©Keith Scott Morton; Page 95—©Keith Scott Morton;

Pages 96-97—©Keith Scott Morton

Mix New and Old
Pages 98-99—©William P. Steele; Page 100—©William P. Steele; Page 101—©Keith Scott Morton; Page 102—©Michael Luppino; Page 103—©Michael Luppino

Modern Country Living
Pages 104-105—©Keith Scott Morton; Page 106—©Keith Scott Morton; Page 107—©Keith Scott Morton; Page 108—©Keith Scott Morton; Page 109—©Keith Scott Morton; Page 110—©Michael Luppino; Page 111—©Michael Luppino Page 112—©Keith Scott Morton; Page 113—©Keith Scott Morton

Eclectic Charm
Pages 114-115—©Keith Scott Morton; Page 116—©Keith Scott Morton; Page 117—©Keith Scott Morton; Page 118—©Keith Scott Morton; Page 119—©Keith Scott Morton; Page 120—©Steve Gross and Sue Daley; Page 121—©Keith Scott Morton

Storage Made Simple
Pages 122-123—©Helen Norman; Page 124—©Helen Norman; Page 125—Courtesy Gridley and Graves; Pages 126-127—Courtesy Gridley and Graves; Page 128—©Keith Scott Morton; Page 129—©Dominique Vorillon; Page 130—©Charles Maraia; Page 131—©Charles Maraia

The Focal Point
Pages 132-133—©Steven Randazzo; page 134—©Keith Scott Morton; Page 135—©Keith Scott Morton; Page 136—©Michael Luppino; Page 137—©Grey Crawford; Page 138—©Grey Crawford; Page 139—©Steven Randazzo; Pages 140-141—©Steven Mays